Post-Nonmonogamy and Beyond

MORE THAN TWO ESSENTIALS

Post-Nonmonogamy and
Beyond

Andrea Zanin

THORNAPPLE PRESS

Post-Nonmonogamy and Beyond
A More Than Two Essentials Guide

Thornapple Press, 300–722 Cormorant Street
Victoria, BC V8W 1P8 Canada press@thornapplepress.ca

Our business offices are located in the traditional, ancestral and unceded territories of the lək̓ʷəŋən and W̱SÁNEĆ peoples. We return a percentage of company profits to the original stewards of this land through South Island Reciprocity Trust. Thornapple Press is a brand of Talk Science to Me Communications Inc. Talk Science is a WBE Canada Certified Women Business Enterprise, a CGLCC Certified 2SLGBTQI+-owned business, and a Certified Living Wage Employer.

Cover and interior design by Jeff Werner; Substantive editing by Eve Rickert; Copy-editing by Heather van der Hoop; Proofreading by Alison Whyte; Cover detail derived from Henri Rousseau, Tropical Forest with Monkeys (1910), public domain, courtesy American National Gallery of Art.

Library and Archives Canada Cataloguing in Publication
Title: Post-nonmonogamy and beyond / Andrea Zanin.
Names: Zanin, Andrea, author.
Description: Series statement: More than two essentials ; 8 | Includes bibliographical references.
Identifiers: Canadiana (print) 20240411900 | Canadiana (ebook) 20240411919 | ISBN 9781990869556 (softcover) | ISBN 9781990869563 (EPUB)
Subjects: LCSH: Non-monogamous relationships. | LCSH: Libido.
Classification: LCC HQ980 .Z36 2024 | DDC 306.84/23—dc23

Digital print edition 1.0

Contents

Acknowledgments

Thanks, merci, gracias

To Mitch and Bennett: For everything, and for the time and space that helped me write this.

To Ben, Katie B., Josh, Erin, Mark, Katie O., Charlie, Mylène: For being wonderful and supportive chosen family. Josh, you're finally gonna get that book launch.

To Alies and Harry: For the valuable feedback, and so much more.

To Eve and Thornapple: For being my first!

To Shelley and Jack: For taking a chance on me a long time ago.

To everyone who's encouraged me to write: It all helped, every single word of it.

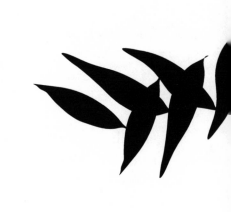

Introduction

Welcome to the post-nonmonogamy discussion group! Grab a coffee and a cookie from the table in the back, if you like, and have a seat. You don't have to participate; you can sit here silently if you want. Maybe there's nothing much to talk about anymore. But we do encourage discussion.

ALL RIGHT, FOLKS, LET'S GET STARTED! Our topic today is: What is post-nonmonogamy?

I'll explain, but first, let me tell you a bit of my story so you know where I'm coming from.

In my twenties, in the golden era of blogging (the early aughts), I started writing about my explorations and studies in the realms of queer sex, gender, kink and nonmonogamy. My blog, *Sex Geek*, brought me a surprising amount of attention for posts such as one positing ten rules for happy nonmonogamy and, later, one in which I articulated and critiqued the concept of polynormativity.[1] I was invited to teach workshops and sit on panels, and eventually to travel the world and speak at conferences. I was actively nonmonogamous—from short-term connections to longer, deeper relationships. For the better part of a decade, into my mid-thirties, I lived in two consecutive triads.

In my thirties, I did a master's degree in gender studies and started a PhD. While I was doing that, the chronic pain I had been experiencing since my early teens rose to the point of being debilitating. I spent years juggling my speaking career, my studies, my freelance work and my multiple relationships while also spending more and more time going to doctors and getting tests and treatments. Eventually, they figured out I had a rare spinal cord tumour. I had surgery. It grew back, and the pain became even more intense. I dropped out of my PhD. My partnerships broke up; I somehow hooked up with someone new, and we were together for many years while I continued to navigate the health system. I had surgery a second time, and radiation, and severe radiation side effects, and treatments for those side effects, and side effects from those treatments.

Eventually, at forty, I wound up single, broke and (what felt like) broken.

I rebuilt. It was excruciatingly slow; sometimes my progress was barely perceptible even to me. But I did it. Over the next few years, I revitalized my lagging freelance career, fixed my finances and clawed my way back to a kind of health I didn't think I would ever achieve again. And throughout it all, I remained single and uninvolved. Mending my heart—after multiple great loves and multiple great heartbreaks—was the slowest fix of all, and some of the fixing lay in learning that, as Olivia Laing writes, "not all wounds need healing, and not all scars are ugly."[2] There came a point in the middle of all that when I began to think about maybe dating. Just maybe. And then COVID-19 arrived.

4

So it feels terribly strange to me that as the world has opened up again, I have begun to be asked once more to teach and write on topics related to nonmonogamy and kink. Who am I to impart any insight at all when I haven't actually done these things in close to a decade? Who am I to write a book for a fresh, exciting series on nonmonogamy? I don't feel fresh and exciting. I feel ancient and jaded, which is kind of like being experienced, only grumpy about it.

But then I realized maybe that's exactly what I had to offer: the perspective of someone who's done a thing or two—and then moved on to other things.

The purpose of this small offering, then—this discussion group in book form—is not to provide guidance on how or why to do nonmonogamy, or

5

not. It's more like glancing around the circle and giving a gentle nod of recognition to those who've done it, and then, for one reason or another, chosen not to do it anymore. Not because of a change of heart about the underlying principle that it's okay to have multiple consensual relationships at the same time; we are post-nonmonogamists, not anti-nonmonogamists. But for … other reasons. We'll get to those shortly.

For some folks, post-nonmonogamy might look like becoming or remaining single. That might be a state you didn't choose but that you embraced, or one that's been deliberate from the start; maybe you've decided to actively invest in your relationship with yourself, along the lines of what author and kink educator Lee Harrington calls "becoming your own beloved."[3] For others, post-nonmonogamy might look like what one of my wise Best Exes calls "monogamy by attrition"—when the number of relationships you're in dwindles down to one and remains there, and you don't seek to change that. For still others, it looks like being alone for a while after a nonmonogamous arrangement ends and then starting a new relationship with just one person. Therapist and author Jessica Fern considers such pathways into a dyadic relationship after a time spent being nonmonogamous to be a choice of exclusivity rather than a default to monogamy.[4] But you're welcome at this meeting whether you consider yourself (happily or otherwise) single, celibate, self-married, quirkyalone,[5] or (happily or otherwise) exclusive or monogamous.

Look around the room. This is an eclectic gathering! Many of you are middle-aged or above, but some are unwrinkled; there's a smattering of students, some parents with phones that will buzz about the babysitter in a couple hours, a few folks in leather vests. People of various genders, races and body types, and quite a number of spoonies, visible or otherwise.[6] Some straight folks, some queers. Glad you could all make it. Thanks ever so kindly for respecting the scent-free policy.

Some of you might be surprised to see just how big this group is. But it makes sense. The latest stats show that at any given time, in both Canada and the United States, 4 to 5 percent of the population is actively nonmonogamous. And the research also shows that somewhere around one-fifth of the US population (no stats exist for Canada) has done some kind of nonmonogamy at some point in their lives.[7] That means that at any given moment,

> At any given time, in both Canada and the United States, 4 to 5 percent of the population is actively nonmonogamous.

there are about three times as many former nonmonogamists as there are current ones. And as nonmonogamy becomes increasingly acceptable and better known, more and more people are doing it ... which means that many more people might one day stop.

Also worth noting: Post-nonmonogamy isn't necessarily a permanent state. You may be post-nonmonogamous now, but later choose to re-enter nonmonogamy after a time of rest and retreat. You can move fluidly into a post-nonmonogamous period, back out of it, and maybe back in. Or you can decide you're done, once and for all. There are no hard-and-fast rules here.

In this book, I explore a set of reasons, broad categories really, that, taken alone or in combination, I think cover much of what might bring a person into post-nonmonogamy. Of course, my framework and my thoughts are based on and filtered through my own experience, which may look nothing like yours. Among other things, I think that for some people, there isn't really a reason for post-nonmonogamy per se; it just worked out that way and felt all right, so they stayed that way. If that's the case for you, my in-depth explorations in chapter 2 might be a little more than you really need, and you may want to skip to chapter 3. But your reasons don't have to fit into my framework to be valid. I hope that this exploration will be useful to you even if your pathway isn't covered here. Perhaps my questions will inspire some

conversations with your loved ones or
with your (one, just one now) partner,
or maybe you'll journal about it or
take it into your next therapy session.
Or hey, you could even create a real
live discussion group of your own!

As a now-sorta outsider with insider
knowledge, as a no-longer practitioner,
as a former-but-possibly-also-future
nonmonogamist—I hope that you
might come out feeling less alone
(even if you're, you know, alone)
and less weird (even if you're weird)
in the space after nonmonogamy
that so many of us inhabit.

On Identity and Choice

In *Nonmonogamy and Happiness*, philosopher Carrie Jenkins looks at one of those questions that regularly comes up in nonmonogamous circles: whether nonmonogamy is a choice or an identity.

JENKINS ARGUES THAT FIXATING ON this question

may be linked to a temptation to *justify* or *excuse* nonmonogamy on the grounds that it is an involuntary and unchangeable condition (because an identity feels more involuntary and unchangeable than a mere preference), and hence the nonmonogamous cannot be blamed for being the way they are. But none of this is necessary. Nonmonogamy requires no excuse of this kind. Identity or not, involuntary or not, there's simply nothing here that needs justification.[8]

I appreciate her point, because frankly, as a queer, I'm incredibly tired of the "nature vs. nurture" debate about sexual orientation, and I really don't like how close this "choice vs. identity" question comes to that same debate. I don't care how I got this way (queer, kinky, nonmonogamous). I don't care whether it's my "fault" or not. The actual problem is the very idea that we should all follow one path, and that we can only ever be one thing in the course of our lives. Besides, there are so many more interesting questions to ask about who we are and what we do. Human diversity, sexual and otherwise, is fascinating!

I'm also pretty bored with the incessant discussion of identity. It's not that identity is unimportant; it can help us understand ourselves, gather together with people who share common ground, shape our thinking into useful lines of inquiry. It's just that identity isn't *everything*. We each share lots of experiences—joyful, oppressive, neutral—with people who don't share our identities.

Jenkins considers "choice vs. identity" to be a false dichotomy, arguing that some identities change, at times voluntarily. I agree, and I want to explore this more deeply for a moment. I think the facts of our lives sometimes line up with words that are technically correct, but that doesn't mean they are identities. For example, a person who loses a spouse may be a widow or widower, but some people build an identity around that fact, while others might never do so. As another example, I was disabled for most of my twenties and thirties, but it took many years before I realized that *disabled* was a word that applied to me, and it took me even longer to develop any kind of identity as a disabled person—there was a great lag between the experience and the self-understanding. Then, a few years into the identity, my medical issues resolved to a point where I became no longer disabled. But I certainly haven't forgotten the many things I learned during the time I spent there, and while I don't claim the label anymore, I feel an affinity for disability issues and disabled folks that I don't think will ever disappear.

And maybe that's why I long to break out of the identity vs. choice dichotomy, or the question of being vs. practising—is nonmonogamy a thing we are, or a thing we do? Does it matter if we stop doing it? If so, for how long? But like any binary, these ones are too simple to contain the vastness we all bring to the table as human beings.

The existentialists insist that we are at choice in every moment, whether we like it or not; as Sartre said, "I can always choose, but I ought to know that if I do not choose, I am still choosing." If we go with that idea, we acknowledge that we can be and do multiple things over the course of our lives, whether we're choosing to allow ourselves to be buffeted by our circumstances or choosing to intervene with as much agency as we can muster. We can understand that while our past choices influence our present options, they don't predetermine the choices we must make in the present.

I love the freedom this mindset opens up. It gives me hope that all of us can change if we want to, that nothing is predetermined. But at the same time, I don't think we are ever free of our pasts. We are built out of stories; we are an amalgamation of the things that have happened to us, the choices we've made, and the meanings we make of each one, whether we articulate them or let them simmer on the back burner of our semiconsciousness. When I say we're built out of stories, I mean that in the sense that storytelling—to ourselves and to others—is important to us as self-reflective and social beings. But also in the concrete, physical sense that our experiences (and our reactions to them) are encoded in our neural pathways, such that we are to an extent literally made out of stories, by way of electrical pulses blazing microscopic channels in the Jello of our brains. So while we are free to make radically different choices from everything we've done before, starting right this minute, it would be delusional to think that what we've done up 'til now can be easily disregarded.

I think identities happen when we look at facts and ask ourselves, "what does this *mean* to me?" The facts themselves may be set in stone, or they may change over time, whether by choice or by circumstance, but regardless, they have only a loose relationship to the ways we make meaning of them. For example, by some logics, I was basically a secular monk for a few years, never mind my long history of living, studying, teaching and building community around sex, nonmonogamy and kink. By others, I was always a kinky nonmonogamous sex freak, just having a long dry spell. Both are true, and neither. It all depends on how I tell the story.

So what happens if you retain all the philosophical, political and emotional underpinnings that led you to nonmonogamy (or that you developed once you got there), all the carefully learned language and skills, all the social networks, all your life experience, and even others' ongoing perception of you as nonmonogamous ... but you just *don't wanna* anymore? The appetite is absent, the drive has disappeared, it just isn't happening.

You are now a post-nonmonogamist.

On Appetite

How did you get here? I think the idea of appetite is key, so let's talk about that a bit. About wanting, desiring, seeking, hungering.

THE PRECONDITION FOR HAVING A relationship is wanting one, or at minimum, being open to one, even just a tiny crack. Sometimes, a sweetness of feeling arrives and trickles its way into the smallest opening, like water into rock; sometimes it feels sudden, like a tectonic heave that shoots a new mountain skyward in a great chaotic mess, destructive and generative all at once. Or perhaps you end up doing the thing before you became aware of wanting to—a soft unfurling of your heart, surprising in its fullness when you turn to look. All these things count as a kind of openness.

Let's look at the more conscious kinds of openness to relationship for a minute. That appetite for connection, that desire or hunger for human contact. It may be a sexual hunger, or it may not; sex is a reliable driving force for seeking partnership, but it's not the only one (greetings, asexual comrades). Companionship, a shared life, even practical projects such as having children—all these and more can drive us in a search for intimate partnership of one kind or another, or inspire us to stay open to it even if we're not actively seeking.

All right. Now, what about the lack of appetite? By this, I mean that whether you're single or partnered with one person, you don't have the desire for the "more" that nonmonogamy brings. I have a theory that most reasons for lack of appetite come down to one or more of the following three scenarios: One, perhaps we don't have a sex drive to speak of, whether temporarily or permanently. Two, perhaps we're dealing with life stress, from everyday saturation all the way up to major trauma, that closes us down to connection. Or, three, perhaps we're simply content in our solitude, or in the web of meaningful but not intimate-partner-y relationships in our world. (I don't have any desire or ability to define what *intimate partner* means,

so please use your own definition
for the sake of this discussion.)

Let's unpack each of these aspects
of lack of appetite for relationship.

On Desire (and Its Absence)

In my twenties, I had a relentless, high
sex drive. It was a glorious, powerful
thing, and it inspired me to seek out all
kinds of knowledge, experiences and
pleasures. In my thirties, my sex drive
was still present, but in the throes of
chronic pain it became difficult to enjoy
my body, whether because my nerves
were misfiring or because the whole
medical system was just so exhausting,
draining on a cellular level. The more
doctors probed and prodded me—from
painful hands-on (or hands-in) pelvic
floor therapy to gory lower-back nerve

block injections, from X-rays to MRIs to Holter monitors to 24-hour urine tests—the less sexy my body felt, and the more tender and fragile. Then radiation accidentally fried my ovaries, and suddenly, at thirty-seven, I was thrust into instant early menopause, and my sex drive disappeared entirely. My sudden radical hormone shift, piled on top of years of medical trauma, pelvic nerve problems and my lengthy experience of the state I call all-touch-is-pain, combined to produce an absolute, bone-deep revulsion toward sex. I couldn't even imagine why people would want it.

Understandably, this was hard on my then-partner, whom I continued to love and find beautiful, but with whom I just could not manage to sustain a sex life. I had gone from being a person with a lot of what sex educator Emily Nagoski calls spontaneous desire,

> Everyone, regardless of what level of sexual desire we feel, can learn a lot from asexual perspectives.

all the way past the other—very common but less well-known—mechanism called responsive desire, to something awfully close to sex-averse asexuality.[9] I stopped short of taking on an ace identity, because to me it felt like my zero-desire state was a response to circumstances rather than a proper orientation. Nevertheless, in recalling that bewildering feeling, I find great solace in the work of brilliant aces such as Sherronda J. Brown, who writes:

What must always be affirmed and reaffirmed is the truth that having rare, absent, or "low" sexual desire is not shameful. It is not an inherent aberration that needs to be urgently fixed—regardless of what the reasons behind it may or may not be, regardless of what other things it might be tangled up with—especially if the methods for "fixing" it come with side effects that negatively impact our actual health, and if the reasons for why we feel the need to "fix" it are due to societal, medical, or interpersonal pressures.[10]

Ultimately, I remain an allosexual person; slowly, my ability to feel desire did grow back, though it took many years, hormone replacement medication, bodywork and a lot of therapy, and it didn't happen until after that relationship ended. But I think everyone, regardless of what level of sexual desire we feel, can learn a lot from asexual perspectives on relationships and connection, because it's very easy to get stuck in a mindset that tells us we'd better want to have sex or we'll never find partnership, and therefore

also never find happiness. There's
a coercive flavour to this mindset,
something lurking and unsavoury,
like a predator at a party. Brown's
term for it is *compulsory sexuality*.

I think of compulsory sexuality as
the electrical system that powers the
"relationship escalator"—essentially,
the societally prescribed approach to
relationships that mandates people
follow a series of predetermined steps
toward achieving a permanent, lifelong
monogamous commitment. According
to author Amy Gahran, sexual connection is one of the five hallmarks of an
escalator relationship, and an escalator
relationship is "what most people grow
up believing (or more accurately, assum-
ing) that intimate relationships 'should'
look like, how they are 'supposed' to
work—and indeed, what any emotionally healthy adult 'should' want."[11]

Gahran argues that while escalator relationships are great for some people, they don't work for everyone. And Brown argues that if we don't make space in society for people to say no to sex, up to and including a permanent and lifelong no, then effectively no sex can truly be consensual. It's strangely appropriate that nonmonogamy and asexuality advocates should converge on questions of consent and relationship diversity. As Brown writes (and doubtless Gahran would agree), "it is imperative that we divest from compulsory sexuality, from the idea that sex is universally desired, that it is the mandatory route to joy and satisfaction, intimacy and connection, emotional intelligence, maturity, sanity, morality, humanity."[12] If, as a society, we were to eschew both compulsory sexuality and the relationship escalator—not necessarily ditching the practice of forming lifelong sexually monogamous commitments for those who want them, but dropping the pressure or obligation to do so and the assumption that we *must* want to—then we would make space for all kinds of other relationships to flourish.

Now, starting from that viewpoint, I want to take a slightly different angle on this question. And that is: While I believe it's important, intellectually and emotionally, to interrogate these social strictures on how people love and form relationships, and to try to make decisions that come from a more authentic and less obedient place, the standard approach of "feel sexual attraction, act on it, and form an intimate relationship as a result" really does work for a lot of people. Asexuals form a tiny fraction of the population; Brown quotes a 2019 study stating that 1.7% of sexual minority adults identify as asexual.[13] That means the vast majority of people still feel sexual desire of some sort. And while non-monogamy is one approach that leads people off the relationship escalator and can make space for nonsexual and not-very-sexual relationships, for a huge swath of humanity, sexual desire is still core to the formation and sustenance of intimate partnership bonds.

Which all adds up to: If you don't want to fuck—at all, or just mostly—you're probably not going to go out of your way to cultivate relationships of the sexual or romantic kind (separately or combined). You may have other motivations for seeking out or continuing to engage in intimate relationships (and for our purposes, in non-monogamy), but this major driver is off the table. And if sexual or romantic attraction is a key element of how you conceive of building intimate partnership, and you're not feeling it, you might not have another sufficiently compelling reason to undertake the process of finding one or more people to get involved with.

If we do the math (could you pass me a napkin, please?), that means that no matter what our sexual and relationship histories look like, and no matter how much space we make

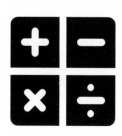

for expanding and redefining every piece of the equation (what is a relationship? what is a partner? what is sex? what is intimacy? what is monogamy? what is nonmonogamy?), if we don't want to have sex, a good number of us may end up in only one

enduring partnership (possibly one
that's no longer very sexual, or never
was), or no longer in partnerships at all.

And thus, lack of sex drive—whether
permanent or temporary—is one factor
that can lead to post-nonmonogamy.

§

I do want to take a moment to note
that if you're unhappy about not feeling
much sexual desire, there are things
you can do about it. You can start by
educating, or re-educating, yourself
about the way desire works. Whether or
not you've been accustomed to having
easy access to your desire, you may be
surprised to learn how many factors
can get in the way of it. A mental
reframe of what's going on might lead
to major insights about the kinds of
solutions that might work for you.

For example, according to Dr. Jen Gunter, the menopause transition is often associated with a decline in desire, but contrary to popular belief, this decline is unrelated to hormone levels (my own experience notwithstanding). Dr. Gunter notes that various other things may be the culprit: genitourinary syndrome of menopause (which can cause pain during sex), medications, medical conditions, poor sleep, depression, incontinence, relationship problems, financial stress, work stress or other stress.[14] Many of these factors apply to people well beyond those going through menopause. We should of course take a cue from Sherronda Brown—"Capitalism is always invested in convincing us that we are flawed in order to sell us remedies"—and be critical about medical and pharmacological imperatives toward normative libido levels, as these are both inextricable from the drive for profit and social normativity.[15] But depending on your situation and what matters most to you, it still might be worth considering whether medical factors might be at play.

Beyond the possibility of medical issues, Lauren Fogel Mersey and Jennifer A. Vencill provide comprehensive advice about handling libido differences across the spectrum of gender and orientation (it's not just a hetero problem!). They point out that

often we find that desire is "low" not because of a physiological issue, but because the sex that folks are having simply isn't all that good! From a sex therapy perspective, the "low" desire in these cases is more accurately a sign of good judgment—after all, who gets excited to have sex that's painful, boring, or generally unsatisfying? [16]

So, if you're partnered and dealing with low desire, consider the possibility that it's worth working on your technique together. Sex isn't necessarily an innate skill; it can be learned and practised. And if you're not partnered but might want to be, don't just count on NRE (new relationship energy) to keep your motor running in your next relationship. Instead, talk openly about what's working and what's not so that you can lay down foundations for satisfying sex in the long run. One thing that can help is taking in Emily Nagoski's fantastic insights about the dual-control model of sexual arousal. She encourages readers to pay attention to both their sexual "accelerators" and their sexual "brakes," otherwise known

as the sexual excitation and sexual inhi-
bition systems.[17] She also explains how
stress can impact a person's sex drive,
how arousal nonconcordance operates,
and more about how to work with
desire discrepancies in relationships.

You may be noticing a theme: Stress
is a gigantic factor in sexual desire. I
think low sex drive is worth considering
on its own as a motivator for post-
nonmonogamy, but the concept of stress
has much broader implications beyond
sex. So let's talk about that next.

On Stress and Trauma

In my early twenties, after two multi-
year abusive relationships in my teens,
I vowed that I would stay single until
I figured out why I kept picking such
shitty partners and how to stop doing

it. It took two years before I trusted myself enough to date. In the ensuing twenty-plus years, I learned that not every abuser is as obvious (in hindsight, of course) as my teenage partners were, but at the time it was still a really positive move. A way to stop myself from making the same mistakes over and over again. A space to heal.

Sometimes, you get burned, and it takes a while to grow your skin back. Perhaps you've exited an abusive or otherwise harmful relationship and you're still reeling from the pain of it all, questioning your ability to judge a person's character or to set and hold boundaries to keep yourself safe. You may blame yourself, or perhaps you're very aware that the abuse wasn't your fault (loud and clear, in case you need to hear this: IT WASN'T), but you still feel reluctant to take further risks or make yourself vulnerable to another human being. Perhaps you weren't abused, but you still got your heart broken or your world shattered. Breakups in general, and nonmonogamous breakups in particular, can be devastating![18] Regardless of the specific contours of your story, the idea of falling in love can sometimes start to look less like a soft-focus movie scene of tumbling into a pillowy bed with a seductive new person, and more like plunging off a cliff to certain agony or death on the rocks below.

In her book *Falling Back in Love with Being Human*, Kai Cheng Thom asks:

Have you ever wondered how human beings can be so contradictory—so cruel and depraved, yet so capable of kindness all at once? Have you ever struggled to hold on to these multiple truths, to your

faith in the possibility of human goodness,
in the face of all the chaos and conflict
that we inflict upon one another?[19]

Such questions, particularly when
applied to intimate relationships, can
cause us to step back. We sometimes
need to nurse ourselves back to health
alone, or in connection with others
who don't fit our personal definition of
"intimate partner." We may opt to stay
unattached, or exclusively attached to
one trusted person, in order to re-find
our centre, to get grounded, to chart out
a new path and make fresh decisions
about how and who we want to be in
our relationships and in the world.

Thom makes some beautiful
suggestions on how to fall back in love
with being human—I interpret these
not so much as trite self-care acts, but
more like poetry in action, pathways

to self-reconnection and hope. "Go into the woods or a nearby park and let yourself take to the earth like a fallen tree," she says. "Cover yourself in flowers, grass, or leaves. Lie on the ground and feel anything you need to feel. When you are ready, rise from the dead and go home. Have a cup of tea."[20] I think once we've found our way back to loving being human, we can also potentially find our way back to (romantically) loving other humans— but all this can take a while. We might need to stay lying on the ground, covered in flowers, for months or years. We might need many, many cups of tea.

§

Abuse, heartbreak and post-relationship recovery are some of the most obvious reasons we might need to step back

from romance to whatever extent,
or choose exclusivity temporarily or
permanently. But they're by far not
the only ones. Sometimes, we are just
too fucking tired. As we all try to
survive under late capitalism, everyday
stress and exhaustion are endemic
for all but the most privileged. From
wage inequality to climate change to
the housing crisis, on top of regular
human things like school, work, or
caring for kids or aging parents, being
alive today is a lot tougher than it
was even just twenty years ago.

Tricia Hersey, in her ringing
manifesto *Rest Is Resistance*, calls for
rest as a form of activism, as a refusal
to dedicate our lives to a set of ideals
that drain our health and well-being,
that sap our ability to dream and
simply exist. "We are in crisis," she
writes. "This rest movement is not some

cute and frivolous idea but instead
an intentional disruption against very
violent systems. It has the potential
to save lives and restore bodies and
minds. It is healing work that will not
be easy."[21] She roots her call for rest
in the history of exploitation of Black
people under slavery, and extends
that need for rest as resistance into
today's culture of endless work.

When I think about grind culture, and
what it has done to my own body, I deepen
into my resistance. When I spend time
processing the manipulation, the scam,
and declaration by grind culture that our
bodies do not belong to us and instead
belong to systems seeking domination
and wealth, it enrages and saddens me.
Collective rest is not about just changing
our individual lives but shifting the entire
paradigm of culture. Our disruption of

capitalism and white supremacy via rest
is to pull back the veil and get behind
the curtain to see everything that has
been told to us about rest, labor, sleep,
leisure, and care has been a lie.[22]

Hersey's activist imperative to rest
comes from her knowledge of history
and from her background in spirituality
and faith. But it also lines up with
the science. Authors and sisters Emily
Nagoski and Amelia Nagoski, in their
book *Burnout,* tell us that we need to
spend 42 percent of our time resting.
"We're not saying you *should* take 42
percent of your time to rest," they write,
"we're saying that if you don't take
the 42 percent, the 42 percent will take
you. It will grab you by the face, shove
you to the ground, put its foot on your
chest, and declare itself the victor."[23]
(Speaking of violent systems...) They

translate this percentage into whatever number of sleep hours you need (for most of us, that's between seven and nine per night) with the remainder devoted to restful activities, exercise, eating and whatever else feels good.

Nonmonogamous people are told—and, if they're not, they learn quickly—that love may be infinite, but time and resources are not. So if we want to be good to the people with whom we're in relationship (and to ourselves), we need to figure out what kind of time we really have, what kind of resources, and how to manage them appropriately. We also need to be honest with ourselves and our partners when these things change.

The balance of each relationship is different and can shift over time: we give, we receive, and sometimes a magical alchemy happens where those two things are one and the same.

Some relationships
contribute to that 42
percent, feeding us in
ways that feel like rest.
Some relationships

> No matter how
> much love we
> feel, we are only
> human: limited

take from us more than they give, and
over time that becomes unsustainable.
No matter how much love we feel,
we are only human: limited.

My big takeaway from *Burnout*
is that if people are being treated as
"human givers" rather than human
beings, or hold themselves to that
expectation, they are more likely to
burn out. If you're a human giver in
your relationships in general, and
you're nonmonogamous, science might
be telling you in no uncertain terms
to stop. But to be clear, even if we're
single, or partnered in a sustainable
and balanced way, we can reach a
point when we realize we cannot add

one more work project, one more hobby, one more obligation—or one more person. We do not all share Tricia Hersey's ancestral connection to generations that suffered some of the worst forms of human exploitation, but very few of us are exempt from grind culture and other elements of what it is to be alive today, and that right there is enough. Olivia Laing writes:

Amidst the glossiness of late capitalism, we are fed the notion that all difficult feelings—depression, anxiety, loneliness, rage—are simply a consequence of unsettled chemistry, a problem to be fixed, rather than a response to structural injustice or, on the other hand, to the native texture of embodiment, of doing time, as [artist] David Wojnarowicz memorably put it, in a rented body, with all the attendant grief and frustration that entails.[24]

In polyamory lingo, we talk about being "polysaturated," meaning we have hit our max capacity for relationships. But—today more than ever—we can also just become saturated by everyday life.

§

Beyond the demands of nonmonogamy and relationships in general, and beyond our swelling levels of everyday life stress, retreat and refusal can feel necessary due to other kinds of stress, too. I'm specifically talking about experiences that rise to the level of trauma. For many people, the desire to be in partnership (or the ability to be present within partnership) drops drastically when they're consumed with overwhelming emotions or cataclysmic life events. Loss and grief are big ones here. Same with handling major health issues, financial disasters or family troubles, or sudden traumatic experiences such as an accident or assault. The big emotions and practical obligations that come with these difficult life experiences can demand all of our energy; we may need every spoon we've got and then some for taking care of ourselves and our immediate problems, and have little left over to seek out or tend to others. The same is true of unravelling long-past experiences of trauma that we haven't yet dealt with. These emotions can take up a lot of space regardless of when the precipitating event happened.

In resilient, flexible relationships, these difficult periods, and our various mechanisms for coping with them, create an ebb and flow over time in which partners support each other and accept the lack of focus for a while, rely on lower-effort ways of connecting until more spoons become available, or simply understand and adapt to the asymmetry as the new normal. In less resilient partnerships, these kinds of high-stress events can hammer at the existing weak spots and cause ruptures or make us see our choices (or our partners) in a different light. Traumatic stress brings some partners closer, but drives others apart. I think people say things like "They broke up because of the accident" as shorthand, but the real story, much of the time, is more like "They broke up because they each handled the trauma of the accident in different ways, which brought to light their incompatibilities."

If major life stresses or traumatic events happen while we're unpartnered or partnered with only one person, they may preclude the effort of finding and building any new partnerships. In any of these cases, the retreat may be temporary, but *temporary* can mean anything from a few weeks to many years. Healing cannot be hurried.

"And what is healing, anyway?" asks Gabor Maté in his masterwork on trauma, *The Myth of Normal*. He answers himself:

When I speak of healing, I am referring to nothing more or less than a *natural movement toward wholeness*. Notice that I do not define it as the end state of being completely whole, or "enlightened," or any similar psychospiritual ideal. It is a direction, not a destination; a line on a map, not a dot.[25]

A direction, a line. One assumes it is jagged, or looping, taking us on side quests and alternate routes. As well as not being quick, healing is rarely a linear process in the sense of being straightforward. And where do we even begin? Therapy and medication are the go-to answers in the present era, but it hasn't always been that way, and these shouldn't be the only things we do now. Trauma researcher Bruce Perry looks to millennia of human history to explain:

The pillars of traditional healing were 1) connection to clan and the natural world; 2) regulating rhythm through dance, drumming, and song; 3) a set of beliefs, values, and stories that brought meaning to even senseless, random trauma; and 4) on occasion, natural hallucinogens or other plant-derived substances used to facilitate healing with the guidance of a healer or elder. It is not surprising that today's best practices in trauma treatment are basically versions of these four things.[26]

Here, Perry is providing a four-part framework to summarize how human beings have traditionally healed from trauma; he criticizes the Western medical model for its overreliance on pharmaceuticals and short-term therapy to the detriment of this more holistic approach. Independently of Perry's framework, these same ideas come up in various forms in much of today's thinking about stress and trauma. Kai Cheng Thom tells us to lie on the forest floor and then rise from the dead and drink tea. Tricia Hersey calls for collective napping. The Nagoski sisters explain how to complete the stress cycle by engaging in physical activity, particularly rhythmic kinds, and creative and musical pursuits. Journalist Jim Rendon summarizes the research on post-traumatic growth, saying that moving from the depths of a traumatic experience to growth requires "deliberately ruminating on the problems, ... narrative reframing, [and] the need for some level of help and support from loved ones."[27] Gabor Maté recounts his experience of profound healing through an Indigenous ayahuasca ritual in the Amazon, which stretches his secular mindset and leaves him grasping for words to describe his breakthrough. All the parts are there, described by artists and scientists, activists and scholars, poets and educators alike. How many of us have access to all four? What would we have to change about our lives—and society—to get there?

Whether or not they each address all four pillars described by Perry, I notice a through line among all the people whose ideas I've been discussing: a call for deep healing as distinct from self-improvement, a call for rest and connection instead of exhaustion and accomplishment, a call to return to humanity and meaningful relationships while refusing the demands of a sick culture and resisting violent systems. What this all adds up to, in my mind, is that it takes time, effort and rest to become well. A kind of slowness, a kind of refusal. A vacation or a spa day is not going to cut it. I'm talking about a profound reorientation of priorities, of how we use the hours we have on this planet.

Art and technology scholar Jenny Odell describes how people often choose a period of removal that fundamentally changes their attitude to the world they return to. "Sometimes that's occasioned by something terrible, like illness or loss, and sometimes it's voluntary, but regardless, that pause in time is often the only thing that can precipitate change on a certain scale," she writes.[28] She touts the benefits of "doing nothing," in the sense of removal and retreat; they include time to repair, the sharpening of our ability to listen and perceive, and "an antidote to the rhetoric of growth."[29] And she insists that "we *absolutely require* distance and time to be able to see the mechanisms we thoughtlessly submit to. More than that…, we need distance and time to be functional enough to do or think anything meaningful at all."[30]

None of these thinkers are looking at nonmonogamy, but it makes so much sense to me that as more and more people recognize how the systems that frame our lives do not have our best interests at heart, and as we begin both wanting to heal from whatever trauma we've experienced and realizing we have the agency to do so, this has to impact

our intimate relationships as well.
If we've invested in nonmonogamy,
perhaps whatever kind of polycule
we're part of can serve as part of the
"clan" of Perry's first pillar, or the "help
and support from loved ones" listed
by Rendon as key to post-traumatic
growth. But not all intimate relationships can serve this way, monogamous
or otherwise, much as we might want
them to. And because nonmonogamy by
its nature involves investing in multiple
people aside from ourselves, that may
be part of what we say no to in order
to take the necessary time and energy
for whatever healing we need to do.

Stress and trauma can give us pause,
change or end our existing relationships,
and make us hesitate to seek out or
remain open to new ones. In this sense,
they can be major factors motivating a
move into post-nonmonogamy—and

the space we find there can give us
exactly the kind of distance and time
we need to heal. Also, when we come
out the other end of our period of
removal, the reflection we've done
and the repair we've made may have
changed our minds about what pursuits
we find meaningful and want to return
to going forward. The "rhetoric of
growth" is an idea people usually
apply to capitalism, but this idea that
more is better can also be found in
some approaches to nonmonogamy.
Post-nonmonogamy can help us
question this idea. There is no single
right answer, but for some people, post-
nonmonogamy may become permanent.

§

Some folks reach a state of post-
nonmonogamy when they remain

totally on board with the value of nonmonogamy and with people's right to self-determine what kinds of relationships they engage in, and after they have invested in doing all manner of emotional work—but still find nonmonogamy too emotionally wrenching to practise. Perhaps this describes you. The (perhaps youthful) nonmonogamous ideals you espoused still ring true, but you're now experienced enough to be able to say "You know what? It just doesn't work for me." Maybe your experiences of nonmonogamy were in themselves damaging; maybe those experiences simply tapped into attachment wounds or revealed an emotional makeup that thrives best in exclusivity. Regardless, you figured it out.

All I have to say here is: much respect to you. It's not easy to step back from an ideal, especially if you had set it up as being one that made you more enlightened than the mainstream. I have a lot of admiration for the courage it takes to achieve this kind of self-knowledge and then act on it. It's truly a form of self-respect in action.

On Contentment in Solitude

Speaking of stress and trauma... when the COVID-19 pandemic hit and the world went into crisis mode in early 2020, for many people the sudden changes to everyday life were wrenching. Lovers were separated by sudden border closures; essential workers, frontline and otherwise, had to choose between risking their lives to make a living and risking their livelihoods to stay alive. My heart also went out to all the parents suddenly trying to homeschool small children and to all the white-collar folks adapting to working on Zoom from their hastily curtained-off or nonexistent home offices. To say nothing of the terrifying numbers of people getting sick and dying. The news was filled with horror.

Given the sheer scope of crisis happening all around me and in the world at large, at first I didn't want to admit … how good the isolation felt.

The tragedies were awful, of course. I saw several deaths in my own circles, as well as friends and loved ones who joined the ranks of those disabled by long COVID. I do not take lightly that devastation, multiplied all over the planet.

But suddenly spending all my time alone? Yes! No social obligations aside from check-in calls with loved ones and, eventually, Zoom parties for which I didn't have to leave the house. No travel logistics, nothing to do but work (from home, as I already had for many years), make delicious meals, rest, write, read books, redecorate, do yoga in the living room, and take long, meandering bike rides along empty streets. I bought myself flowers, as Miley Cyrus suggests. It was blissful. It kept being blissful even when my hair grew to unseemly lengths and I didn't touch another human being for months at a time. I just never stopped enjoying my solitude. It was nourishing, replenishing. It enabled a level of self-care that I didn't even know was possible.

I'm not saying I never got lonely. But loneliness was the mosquito bites you endure as you hike the vastness of a magnificent forest, the shoreline of pointy pebbles you pick your way through to enjoy a bracing swim in a bright lake, the cramped plane seat you accept as part of the cost of exploring spectacular locales. It was, in short, a minor annoyance greatly outweighed by the joys of the experience.

I missed touch, too, but not nearly as much as I'd expected to. Maybe it was all the cycling and yoga, my cushy bed and cozy couch, the ability to microwave a hot pack for my back or take a bath. I invested in an acupressure mat bristling with tiny plastic spikes that, once gingerly laid upon, produced the euphoric feeling that often follows an intense massage. I masturbated, but not very much; it didn't feel urgent. I was content.

My contentment in solitude was an extension of my pre-pandemic choices to create a more manageable existence for myself. After my globetrotting polyamorous twenties and my pain-filled, polyamorous but much less adventuresome thirties, in my forties I needed a fucking break. Smaller carbon footprint, smaller scope of focus, smaller life. I had already done the work to get comfortable being alone, and the pandemic just let me luxuriate there.

I didn't start out comfortable. The way I explained my singlehood for a while, when I was feeling bitter and flip, was to say "I'm nonmonogamous, I just hate everyone." My ongoing flirtation with misanthropy has at times been a strange solace. (*Nonmonogamy and Misanthropy* was my original working title for this book, but they told me it wouldn't sell.) As a nonbinary queer kinky nonmonogamous person, it gave me a certain perverse thrill to say "I could, in theory, have a sexual relationship with just about anyone who wanted to, in just about any way, but I'd rather stay home and read a book." (Or write one.)

In my forties I needed a fucking break.

Of the three main pathways to post-nonmonogamy that I'm positing in this book, being less interested in sex might not be a happy thing for many people, and stress and trauma are almost by definition unhappy experiences, even if they teach us valuable lessons or lead to eventual growth. I'd like to argue here that contentment in solitude is the happiest of the three, even though, for many people—certainly for me—it might take a little work to get there. (It might also follow on one or both of the other two, as it did for me.)

§

It's difficult to research the concept of contentment in solitude, because we can come at it from so many different angles. As I see it, our individual picture of contentment in solitude lies at the intersection of at least eight axes. Four of them are about the practicalities of what our solitude looks like:

- sex vs. celibacy

- being in relationship vs. being single

- living with others vs. living alone

- high-intensity vs. low-intensity social, professional, community or family life.

And four involve our emotional state:

- general mental health status

- prioritizing vs. deprioritizing
  self-relationship, introspection
  and self-knowledge

- comfort, familiarity and pleasure
  in solitude vs. discomfort, unfa-
  miliarity and fear of solitude

- high vs. low tendency to feel lonely.

That complexity is beyond my
capacity to map on a diagram, so I
won't even try, but you can imagine that
the possible combinations are nearly
endless. For example, someone could
be single, but live with roommates,
have a busy social life, have lots of
no-strings-attached sex, dislike solitude,
deprioritize self-relationship, and
feel a great deal of loneliness. And
certainly, a person can be crushingly
lonely even while in an intimate

relationship; sometimes we feel loneliness most acutely when partnered, when someone is right next to us yet the connection we want is out of reach.

That's a very different situation from that of someone who is in a relationship and has some sex, but lives alone, has a low-intensity social life, loves their solitude, prioritizes their self-relationship, and feels little loneliness. Some people are truly cut out for solitude. Anneli Rufus, author of *Party of One: The Loner's Manifesto*, says that non-loners "can't stand to be alone. They squirm. They feel ashamed. They yearn for company when they're alone. They're bored and don't know what to do. They're lonely. *We're* not."[31] Meanwhile, I saw desperate-sounding memes circulating on social media once we hit the second or third month of pandemic stay-at-home mandates, exhorting people to "Check on your extrovert friends! They're having a really rough time right now!"

You could switch up any of these variables and emerge with a totally different picture. Society tends to make a lot of assumptions about how these variables group together; for instance, the stereotype of the lonely, unhappy single person living alone, and the stereotype of the social butterfly who can't settle down. But the truth is, for most of us, the mix is anything but stereotypical, and the challenges we must surmount to reach contentment are different depending on our individual mix.

I don't pretend to have solutions to offer, or advice on how to find contentment. I think, though, that if you consider where you fall on each of the axes listed above, you may discover the places that are most challenging for you, and that might help you identify where to focus your effort so that solitude transforms into a place you find appealing.

§

Let's look at the question of loneliness.

Daniel Schreiber, in his beautiful book *Alone*, wrestles with the question of being single in the long term, having always assumed he would end up in a lifetime partnership. He discusses the idea of ambiguous loss—the experience of mourning something you never had, such as a dream partnership or children. He questions whether substituting friendships for this loss of never-was partnership is really the right approach; he questions whether endless, potentially baseless hope is the right emotion to feel. He lands on something beyond these initial instincts for "solving" loneliness and the ambiguous loss of a fantasized future. "Our task then is to accept this ambiguity and, in this acceptance, to look for new possibilities for ourselves," he writes. "Even though ambiguous losses can be traumatic, we are still able to shape our lives, live them fully and find contentment."[32]

That Schreiber codes a partnerless life as an ambiguous loss makes sense to me, in that if you're not someone who actively chose to be alone, it's almost inevitable that you might spend some time wondering about what could have been. Maybe that person you made eye contact with at the corner store that one time was really your soulmate, and the missed connection can never be recaptured. Maybe, if you'd turned left instead of right, taken a morning flight instead of an afternoon one, accepted that dinner party invitation ... who's to say? Of course, for some, a partnerless life is not an ambiguous loss, but a concrete one: a breakup you maybe could have prevented (or chose, but wish you hadn't had to), a decision you regret, a death you mourn.

I personally take a pragmatic view these days. I no longer believe in the concept of a soulmate. I think interpersonal chemistry is a real thing, and so is love. But taking those as starting points, I think it's up to us to make choices: to invest generously or be frugal with our hearts, to be vulnerable or keep our guard up, to heal and improve ourselves in ways that make us better partners or to stay stuck in patterns that hurt (usually ourselves as well as our partners), to ask for what we need or to sit and fume about not getting it, to set boundaries or to keep quiet and let others decide for us, to listen deeply or to wait for the other person to shut up so we can speak. Apply enough goodwill and skill, and you can do spectacular things with the basic ingredients of chemistry and care that aren't nearly as uncommon as many cultural myths would have us believe. Refuse to, and no amount of passion will be enough to create long-term stability. A solid partnership is built on choices and actions; chemicals and feelings only kickstart the process.

Holding this position doesn't mean I think partners are available for the plucking like fruits on a tree; there are still elements of chance, readiness, even magic at play. But it does mean I'm not likely to waste my energy wondering about the what-ifs. I'm more interested in the what-you-make-of-its, whenever they may come. Maybe this practicality is my own resolution to

the problem of the ambiguous loss
represented by unexpected singlehood.
I also take to heart Olivia Laing's view:

I don't believe the cure for loneliness
is meeting someone, not necessarily. I
think it's about two things: learning how
to befriend yourself and understanding
that many of the things that seem to
afflict us as individuals are in fact a result
of larger forces of stigma and exclusion,
which can and should be resisted.[33]

"Befriending yourself" sounds a lot
like what I did during the early pandemic. It became profoundly joyful and
satisfying, so much so that partnership
stopped seeming like it would be a
better option. Would another person
make choices that work for me from the
list I just gave? Rather than wondering
about missed connections, I wondered

about whether "successful" connection would be worth the potential headache. Good chemistry can be a trap, and love can keep us hooked even when someone's not a great match. I know this from experience. The peace and stability of solitude was so much simpler.

Meanwhile, my wide social circle—family, friends populating various concentric circles of closeness, and the far-flung connections of online acquaintanceships—reminded me all the time that I'm not alone in the everyday afflictions I endure. I'm not that special or unique. Whatever I'm going through, others are too—including loneliness. Laing writes, "Loneliness is collective; it is a city. As to how to inhabit it, there are no rules and nor is there any need to feel shame, only to remember that the pursuit of individual happiness does not trump or excuse our obligations to each [other]."[34] I don't think this is the same as placing all our hopes for emotional fulfilment on friendships, as Schreiber would caution against; rather, it's about reminding ourselves that we are not alone in our loneliness when it arises.

Speaking of cities, I'm intrigued by author Rebecca Traister's idea that cities can, in a sense, keep us company and even substitute for a romantic relationship. "Cities allow us to extract some of the transactional services that were assumed to be an integral, gendered aspect of traditional marriage and enjoy them as *actual* transactional service, for which we pay," she writes. "This dynamic also permits women to function in the world in a way that was once impossible, with the city serving as spouse, and sometimes, true love."[35] If something as concrete yet not-human as a city can be a true love (and, I would argue, not only for women), why not other things, such as a deeply engaging career, a penchant for world travel, a meaningful volunteer commitment, a devotion to learning or sport or art? I don't mean to dismiss the reality of loneliness here. Only to argue that many things can keep it somewhere between minimal and manageable, and that it need not rule our lives or decisions.

Let's not forget, too, that loneliness is not necessarily a result of being alone. Sometimes we feel it most keenly when we're surrounded by people, or entwined in relationship. There's nothing quite like that feeling of slippage, that chilly hollowness, when you become aware that you're at once a part of what's going on and also utterly separate from it—and nobody else can tell. In fact, being alone is sometimes the solution to loneliness; when we're all by ourselves, there's nothing from which to feel apart, so we can get about the business of wrapping ourselves in the softness of solitude, appreciating the texture and heft of it, and deciding what to do with all that rich, silky material.

§

While "loners," as Rufus calls them, probably have an easier time overall adjusting to solitude, we can all stand to learn the skill sets. To this end, author Sara Maitland, in *How to Be Alone*, provides a thoughtful, step-by-step program on how to rebalance both society's attitude toward solitude and our own relationship to it, from facing the fear of solitude to finding its joys, and from there, teaching future generations that solitude is beneficial. It's a wonderful little book, full of suggestions for ways to ease into the joy of solitude. Baby steps include learning something by heart; advanced practitioners might take long trips alone or even achieve solo world records. To explain the value of undertaking such a program, she writes:

Even those who know that they are best and most fully themselves in relationships (of whatever kind) need a capacity to be alone, and probably at least some occasions to use that ability. If you know who you are and know that you are relating to others because you want to, rather than because you are trapped (unfree), in desperate need and greed, because you fear you will not exist without someone to affirm that fact, then you are free. Some solitude can in fact create better relationships, because they will be freer ones.[36]

The joys of solitude are many; the potential benefit to our relationships is only one of them. Michael Harris, in his book about refusing the constant stream of social media, writes that choosing mental solitude "is a disruptive act, a true sabotage of the schemes of ludic loop engineers and social media barons. Choosing solitude is a gorgeous waste."[37] I'm not sure I agree that solitude is a waste of any kind, but it is gorgeous. And when constant connection is intended to profit megacorporations, I can see what he means.

I have an easier time getting on board with Harris's concept of solitude as an opportunity for deep but unstructured thinking. He describes the work of a researcher who argues that "the rush of pleasure we get from an 'aha moment' is the equivalent of an orgasm for the thinking mind," and argues that "if we've evolved to take great pleasure from the moment when fresh connections are forged, then letting our mind wander is no longer a guilty indulgence—it is crucial to our success and survival. Our blueprint demands it."[38] This is the pleasure of dreaming and daydreaming (as Tricia Hersey would have us do), of deep listening (Jenny Odell), of reading for both leisure and study, of what I call "personal edification projects," of aimless journaling, of films and music and making art, and—yes, unpredictably, and all the more delicious for it—of the sudden exquisite, electric flash of thoughts coming together in new ways and ideas being born. (Here I am picturing that old *Muppets* skit of the Koozebanian mating ritual, in which two alien creatures reproduce by galloping at each other at full speed across a planet's cratered surface and crashing together like cars; when the smoke clears, both parents have disappeared, and a clutch of peeping young is left in their place.)[39]

Lee Harrington, in turn, sees solitude as an opportunity for self-knowledge. He writes, "when we don't know someone, even if that someone is ourselves, it's easier to ignore their needs, wants, dreams, and desires. It is time that each of us got to know our Self."[40] For Harrington, this is a crucial element of self-partnering, which I think is a great way to reframe the concept of being single. For the nonmonogamous, self-partnering might not exclude the possibility of also partnering with others, but it does foreground the importance of our relationship to ourselves, which I think is essential either way.

§

Let's focus on single folks for a moment. "People who consciously choose to not be partnered are embracing a truly alternative relationship structure," Harrington writes. "They are the ones who have the courage to say that they are enough, that they love themselves, that they choose to be fully present with themselves and all that they are."[41] But even if you don't choose to self-marry or understand yourself as your own beloved, the research shows that single people are often very happy that way.[42]

I've been discussing contentment in solitude, here, as a motivation for post-nonmonogamy. And in that context, I think it's important to acknowledge the value and pleasure of remaining single, perhaps permanently. (Of course, you might also get to this point without ever having been nonmonogamous, but that's a different book!) But I'm not necessarily here to vaunt the merits of singlehood or sell it as a life choice, just as I have always refused to tell anyone that nonmonogamy is the one true way to happiness. Mostly, I just think single life should be destigmatized even more than it already has. Asexuality is not the only way to refuse compulsory sexuality, and nonmonogamy is not the only way to step off the relationship escalator. The choice to live a meaningful single life—or to make an unchosen single life meaningful—is valid and beautiful, even if it's also challenging. (Partnership is challenging too, after all!)

Regardless of our individual reasons for enjoying it, solitude can be a wonderful experience, even in its extremes. You don't need to be a monk to value a simple, unadorned life largely spent alone, and you also don't need to spend your life largely alone to appreciate some sweet solitude when you get the opportunity for it. Just as the starkness of a desert belies the teeming plant and animal life that call it home, there is great vitality and beauty to be found in solitude. As poet Tanya Davis writes:

Alone is a freedom that breathes
    easy and weightless
and lonely is healing if you make it.[43]

On Life after Nonmonogamy

Let's return to our earlier question of identity versus practice.

IF YOU'RE A "NONMONOGAMY AS IDENTITY" person, you may feel like nonmonogamy is so intrinsic to who you are that it applies no matter what you're actually doing at a given time—akin to a sexual orientation that remains real even if you're single or celibate. If you're a "nonmonogamy as choice" person, you may feel like you could choose to do nonmonogamy at some points in your life, but it's equally possible you'll choose to be monogamous or single at other points, and right now is one of those times. In either case, "post-non-monogamous" might be technically true for you, but you can choose to write your narrative in any number of ways. Maybe this book gives you a handy new identity label to embrace, or maybe not. (You're welcome in the group either way!)

How are you telling *your* story?

When you have a nonmonogamous history, as long as the experience of nonmonogamy was meaningful to you and more than fleeting, I'd argue that there's likely to be a qualitative difference in how you approach other relationships—all kinds of relationships—going forward. I don't think most people can expand their thinking in the way that nonmonogamy requires and then just revert back to their previous shape once their mind is no longer being actively stretched. The imprint remains. There are things you can't un-know: the sensation of three mouths sharing a kiss, the delight of conspiring with one partner to surprise another, the feeling of love by extension when you help a metamour move house, the felt experience of compersion when your love is off loving someone else. Insert your own experiences here. The challenging bits, too, where you learn to cope with your own jealousy or handle conflict in new ways.

When we become nonmonogamous, many of us experience what therapist Jessica Fern calls a "paradigm shift," or perhaps a shift in several different paradigms.[44] What those are, specifically, will be different for each person depending on what messages we were taught about how relationships work, what monogamy means, how to show commitment and love, what good communication looks like, and so on. For some of us, the shift into nonmonogamy feels like the tumblers of a lock all clicking into place: Aha! Finally, the right combination, and now everything has opened up! For others, it's more like a process of unlearning and relearning over time, or of making it through a really tough period with useful insights that unfold in the end.

I'm not saying nonmonogamy is all feathers and fabulousness—far from it. I'm saying that, wonderful or difficult, it teaches us things that we don't simply forget or discard when our situation changes. When someone becomes a nonpractising nonmonogamist, two negatives don't make a positive. The arc of your own paradigm shifts may translate, sometime down the line, into the contours of your post-nonmonogamy. What did you specifically unlearn or learn when you entered nonmonogamy? What were your key "aha" moments? What are your strongest memories of times when a new way of being and relating came into focus?

Maybe you dreaded the day that jealousy would come along and clobber you—only to realize that as long as everyone was honest with you, you rarely felt jealous. Perhaps, then, you'll bring that self-knowledge with you as you move into post-nonmonogamy: You tend to function best and feel safest when everyone expresses themselves straightforwardly. And it really helps with the FOMO when your friends get together and you can't join them, for instance, if you know you'd rather see their photos from the camping trip than feel like it's a dirty secret they can't talk about with you.

Maybe you discovered that collaboration is a really strong value for you. That time when you and your partner and your metamour sat down and hammered out the details of how to manage a complicated housing and child care situation showed you that pooling your skills and resources with a group of like-minded people, all on the same team, helped you solve some problems that you might never have figured out alone. You might carry this knowledge with you into post-nonmonogamy, and use it in the workplace where you and your colleagues have to think outside the box to handle an unexpected situation.

Your paradigm shifts are your own, and thus, so is the shape they

> **Your paradigm shifts are your own, and thus, so is the shape they have carved out in the landscape of your life.**

have carved out in the landscape of your life, which in turn informs what your post-nonmonogamy might look like. Whether you choose solitude or an exclusive relationship, what do you retain from your experience in nonmonogamy?

Perhaps it's the communication skills. Your journal entries are erudite, your introspection profound. Your therapist praises your insights and jokes "You don't even need me anymore!" (You know better than to think they mean it.) You handle your relationships with friends, family and colleagues with generosity and expansiveness (and maybe with more than the average amount of processing). You make room for everyone to state their needs and you articulate your own like a pro. You seek out both-and solutions rather than either-or ones at work and in your social world. You've done this. You know how it works.

Maybe you apply your kitchen table polyamory philosophy to your relationships with your roommates or kids. Maybe your sex-positive nonmonogamy-based outlook informs how you counsel a friend who's considering whether to marry their partner, or who's thinking of breaking up, or who's navigating a long-distance relationship. Maybe you've got an uncommonly large network of friends in multiple cities, a communal-use policy for your backyard, a fondness for potlucks. Maybe you roll your eyes at movie plots that rely on the "which person to pick" trope because come on already, that's

such a last-millennium plot device!
(Picture the "why not both?" gif here.)

Maybe you and your partner share
a knowing glance when someone walks
by whom one of you would consider
attractive. Maybe you still share your
colour-coded online calendars even
though you've just got two people's
schedules to coordinate now and not
five. Maybe your mutual ex still has a
set of housekeys and comes over for tea
and conversation sometimes. Maybe
your reminiscences, as a couple, still
include past partners whose time with
one or both of you coincided with your
relationship, for better or for worse.
Maybe both of you get annoyed when
that judgmental relative at the holiday
gathering says "Well, I'm glad the two
of you grew up and settled down and
gave up that polygamy nonsense!"

However nonmonogamy shaped you, whatever skills or perspectives it has left you with, you're always going to see the world through a different lens than if you had never questioned monogamy or stepped into a different way of seeing and doing relationships in the first place.

§

The tenth rule, from my long-ago blog post on ten rules for happy nonmonogamy, is "go with the flow." What I wrote, then, was this:

In other words, don't go out looking for anything. The best people show up when we're just going about our business, doing good things in life, being happy, and being generous. It's not that personals sites or matchmaking are a bad idea ... it's simply that the joy of non-monogamy is in being open to the many things that may come our way, rather than gunning for any one thing in particular. Life is generous if we're open to receiving it, and it pulls away when we clutch at it...a lot like people.

To me, that "go with the flow" philosophy encompassed the spirit of nonmonogamy beyond the concrete aspects of practising it. I was trying to express that nonmonogamy wasn't just about multiple partnerships; it was about a way of thinking rooted in openness, generosity, reciprocity and communication. I was trying to convey the feeling, the vibe of it, beyond the how-to techniques. The way we must learn to embrace that we're not in control of other people or situations. The beautiful paradox that dealing with the people we love in an open-hearted and open-handed way is often the best way to retain connection with them. The ever-greater need—both interpersonally and in the sense of social justice—to co-create solutions with everyone affected by a problem, and to invent new approaches and frameworks rather than imposing rigid, pre-established ones.

I know that not everyone who does nonmonogamy thinks this way, but for me it was absolutely key, even intrinsic. I'm not sure, looking back, whether this set of values is what made me nonmonogamous, or if the nonmonogamy helped me shape this set of values. But I do know that, then and now, a philosophy of openness applies to tons of places beyond the simple question of how many people we're dating at a given time.

While I left nonmonogamous relationships behind me, and then

left partnership behind me entirely—
through a fluctuating sex drive, plenty
of trauma and healing, and a discovery
of pure contentment in solitude—I
think this aspect of nonmonogamy
is the one that will never disappear
for me. The way I put openness into
practice may look very different,
alone in my living room, than it did
when I was living in a triad-anchored
polycule spread across two houses.
But it's still there, still informing how
I think about ... well, everything.

This is what makes me a
post-nonmonogamist.

My ten rules were a joke. I mean,
they are real rules in some ways, but
mostly they're a framework through
which I tried to invite people to ask
themselves a lot of big questions
about their own values, desires,
skills and dreams. In that same

spirit, before we fold up the chairs
and head home, I'll wrap this up by
asking you some new questions:

- Are you a post-nonmonogamist?
  If so, what kind?

- If not, how would you describe your
  position relative to nonmonogamy
  at this point in your life?

- Either way, how did you get there?

- How has your history of nonmonogamy informed who you are
  today and how you do things in life?

- What did you learn from
  nonmonogamy?

- What did you unlearn within it?

- What have you forgotten?

- What are you glad you left behind?

- If you're single, would you ever enter
  partnership again? Why or why not?
  How or how not? When and when not?

- If you're partnered, how does
  your past nonmonogamy affect
  your current relationship?

- Would you ever practise nonmonogamy
  again? Why or why not? How or
  how not? When and when not?

- What resonated for you in this little
  book, and what didn't? Why?

- What other questions do you
  want to be asked? What do
  you want to ask yourself?

Wherever you are in your journey—into or through nonmonogamy, possibly out the other end of it and into post-nonmonogamy, or maybe even considering going back in—I hope you find comfort, connection, nourishment and pleasure there.

§

(I imagine us lingering after the meeting as we sweep up, erase the whiteboard and nosh on the broken bits left behind on the cookie plate. You tell me a bit more of your story. I tell you a bit more of mine.)

Often, when someone asks me what my book is about and I tell them, I see recognition light up in their eyes: "I'm totally post-nonmonogamous!" They're running around after two toddlers while trying to schedule their mother's live-in care, get the dog to the vet and meet a work deadline; they barely have time for sex with their spouse, and the idea of adding anyone else into the mix is ludicrous. They feel like they've aged out of the dating scene and can't bear the thought of rejoining the miserable grind of dating apps, and also, they don't drink anymore. They're like the doctor I had a vaccination appointment with once, who, after quizzing me about my sex life, smiled brightly and said "Oh, I get it, you're like, technically poly, but who has the time, right?"

As I settle into middle age and eyeball the arrival of my fifties just around the next bend, my willingness to put a lot of energy into multiple intimate relationships recedes ever further into my past. A pleasant memory, but exhausting to consider in the present. Instead, I get together for dinner with my Best Exes, or go on vacation with them; I finished writing this book while the three of us were on a multi-week trip to Mexico, checking out art museums and hiking to see rock formations in the mountains.

And then I go home alone. I'm with Daniel Schreiber, who writes, "I enjoy following the seasonal changes of my daily rhythms and not having to account for them to anyone."[45] My yoga practice is far more appealing than a Leather conference; my books, far more alluring than a speed dating event.

Am I open to partnership? Maybe. But pickings are ever slimmer as I age, and my standards have only gotten higher, so it seems mathematically unlikely. A beloved aunt tells me, "It just takes one person, though," and she's right. What I don't tell her is that I'm more interested in

the idea of hopping into bed with
a cute couple every once in a while
than I am in pursuing a serious
relationship of any kind. And I'm
not actually *looking* for even that.

Still, I suppose you never know
what's in store. Post-nonmonogamy is
everywhere, and it can be many things.
It may yet be many more things for me.

What will it be for you?

Notes

1   Polynormativity is the notion that, if a person is
    going to pursue polyamory, they should or must
    follow the one normal, right and expected kind of
    polyamory for which mononormative society has
    made a little space. This type of polyamory starts
    with a couple opening up, is always hierarchical,
    involves a lot of rules, and—in terms of media
    representation—usually looks like a white,
    heterosexual-ish couple with a girlfriend on the side.

2   Olivia Laing, *The Lonely City: Adventures in the
    Art of Being Alone* (New York: Picador, 2016), 280.

3   Lee Harrington, *Become Your Own Beloved: A
    Guide to Delighting in Self-Connection* (New
    York: Twin Flame, 2023).

4   Jessica Fern, Eve Rickert and David Cooley,
    "Jessica Fern, David Cooley and Eve Rickert
    Discuss *Polywise*," YouTube video, at 48:19
    mark, September 27, 2023, https://youtu.be
    /Odbv1WA_-dY.

5   According to author Sasha Cagen, a quirkyalone
    is "a person who enjoys being single (but is not
    opposed to being in a relationship) and generally
    prefers to be alone rather than date for the sake
    of being in a couple." Cagen, "Quirkyalone: A
    Manifesto for Uncompromising Romantics," *Sasha
    Cagen Coaching*, https://www.sashacagen.com
    /quirkyalone.

6   "Spoon theory" was developed by writer and
    blogger Christine Miserandino in 2003 as a way
    of describing the way many disabled people
    have to ration their energy, with units of energy
    symbolized by spoons. While the concept has been
    widely adopted, people who refer to themselves as
    "spoonies" usually mean they are disabled in ways
    that require energy rationing. See Miserandino,
    "The Spoon Theory," *ButYouDon'tLookSick
    .com*, https://butyoudontlooksick.com/articles
    /written-by-christine/the-spoon-theory.

7   Elisabeth A. Sheff, "Updated Estimate of
    Number of Non-Monogamous People in U.S.,"
    Psychology Today, May 27, 2019, https://www
    .psychologytoday.com/us/blog/the-polyamorists-
    next-door/201905/updated-estimate-number-non
    -monogamous-people-in-us.

8   Carrie Jenkins, *Nonmonogamy and Happiness*
    (Victoria, BC: Thornapple Press, 2023), 93.

9   Emily Nagoski, *Come As You Are: Revised and Updated: The Surprising New Science That Will Transform Your Sex Life* (New York: Simon & Schuster, 2021).

10 Sherronda J. Brown, *Refusing Compulsory Sexuality: A Black Asexual Lens on Our Sex-Obsessed Culture* (Berkeley, CA: North Atlantic Books, 2022), 82.

11 Amy Gahran, "What Is the Relationship Escalator?" *Off the Relationship Escalator,* https://offescalator.com/what-escalator.

12 Brown, *Refusing Compulsory Sexuality*, 172.

13 Brown, *Refusing Compulsory Sexuality*, 73.

14 Dr. Jen Gunter, *The Menopause Manifesto: Own Your Health with Facts and Feminism* (Toronto, ON: Random House Canada, 2021), 194–195.

15 Brown, *Refusing Compulsory Sexuality*, 70.

16 Lauren Fogel Mersey and Jennifer A. Vencill, *Desire: An Inclusive Guide to Navigating Libido Differences in Relationships* (Boston, MA: Beacon Press, 2023), 18–19.

17 Nagoski, *Come As You Are,* 47–48.

18 See Eve Rickert and Andrea Zanin, "Relationship Transitions," chapter 21 in *More Than Two, Second Edition: Cultivating Nonmonogamous Relationships with Kindness and Integrity* (Victoria, BC: Thornapple Press, 2024).

19 Kai Cheng Thom, *Falling Back in Love with Being Human: Letters to Lost Souls* (Toronto, ON: Penguin Canada, 2023), 3.

20 Thom, *Falling Back in Love*, 125.

21 Tricia Hersey, *Rest Is Resistance: A Manifesto* (New York: Little, Brown Spark, 2022), 78.

22 Hersey, *Rest Is Resistance*, 79.

23 Emily Nagoski and Amelia Nagoski, *Burnout: The Secret to Unlocking the Stress Cycle* (New York: Ballantine Books, 2019), 168.

24 Laing, *The Lonely City*, 280–81.

25 Gabor Maté with Daniel Maté, *The Myth of Normal: Trauma, Illness & Healing in a Toxic Culture* (Toronto, ON: Knopf Canada, 2023), 362.

26 Bruce D. Perry and Oprah Winfrey, *What Happened to You? Conversations on Trauma, Resilience, and Healing* (New York: Flatiron Books, 2021), 200.

27 Jim Rendon, *Upside: The New Science of Post-Traumatic Growth* (New York: Touchstone, 2015), 132.

28 Jenny Odell, *How to Do Nothing: Resisting the Attention Economy* (Brooklyn, NY: Melville House, 2020), 9–10.

29 Odell, *How to Do Nothing*, 22, 23 and 26.

30 Odell, *How to Do Nothing*, 60.

31 Anneli Rufus, "Party of One," *Anneli Rufus*, http://www.annelirufus.com/partyofone.

32 Daniel Schreiber, *Alone*, trans. Ben Fergusson (London: Reaktion Books, 2023), 120.

33 Laing, *The Lonely City*, 281.

34 Laing, *The Lonely City*, 281.

35 Rebecca Traister, *All the Single Ladies: Unmarried Women and the Rise of an Independent Nation* (New York: Simon & Schuster, 2016), 83.

36 Sara Maitland, *How to Be Alone* (London: Macmillan, 2014), 142.

37 Michael Harris, *Solitude: A Singular Life in a Crowded World* (Toronto, ON: Anchor Canada, 2017), 74.

38 Harris, *Solitude*, 55.

39 "The Muppet Show: Koozebanian Mating Ritual," YouTube video, 2:36, from *The Muppet Show,* season 1, episode 7, posted by "dorcm1973," April 3, 2009, https://www.youtube.com/watch?v=vbXzpoH6m2c.

40 Harrington, *Become Your Own Beloved*, 14.

41 Harrington, *Become Your Own Beloved*, 16–17.

42 Eric Klinenberg, *Going Solo: The Extraordinary Rise and Surprising Appeal of Living Alone* (Richmond, UK: Gerald Duckworth & Co Ltd, 2013).

43 Tanya Davis, with illustrations by Andrea Dorfman, *How to Be Alone* (New York: HarperCollins, 2013), n.p.

44 Jessica Fern with David Cooley, *Polywise: A Deeper Dive into Navigating Open Relationships* (Victoria, BC: Thornapple Press, 2023).

45 Schreiber, *Alone*, 53.

About the

MORE THAN TWO® ESSENTIALS SERIES

More Than Two Essentials is a series of books by Canadian authors on focused topics in nonmonogamy. It is curated by Eve Rickert, author of *More Than Two, Second Edition: Cultivating Nonmonogamous Relationships with Kindness and Integrity*.

Learn more at morethantwo.ca.

**Nonmonogamy and
Neurodiversity**

**Nonmonogamy and
Death**

**Nonmonogamy and
Happiness**

**Nonmonogamy and
Teaching**

How Do I Sexy?
A Guide for Trans and
Nonbinary Queers

Mx. Nillin Lore, with a foreword by
Sophie Labelle

"Nillin's warmth, humor, and
adventurousness are a shining light in
the sex writing community. They live
their queer, pervy life proudly, and in
doing so, inspire others to be truer to
themselves too. Reading their work
serves as a wonderful reminder that sex
is best when infused with fun, freedom,
self-knowledge and self-expression."
— Kate Sloan, author of *101 Kinky
Things Even You Can Do*

Say More: Consent
Conversations for Teens

Kitty Stryker, with a foreword by
Heather Corinna

"*Say More* will change the game for
many young people and parents,
whether dealing with extreme
situations or the everyday challenges
of interpersonal relationships and
maintaining one's agency."
— Alex Winter, actor, *Bill & Ted's
Excellent Adventure*

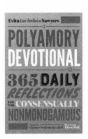

A Polyamory Devotional: 365 Daily Reflections for the Consensually Nonmonogamous

Evita Sawyers, with a foreword by Chaneé Jackson Kendall and illustrations by Tikva Wolf

"Empathetic, witty and engaging, *A Polyamory Devotional* is accessible to people new to polyamory, as well as those who are long-time nonmonogamists."
    — Dr. Elisabeth "Eli" Sheff, author of *The Polyamorists Next Door and Children in Polyamorous Families*

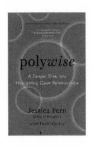

Polywise: A Deeper Dive into Navigating Open Relationships

Jessica Fern, with David Cooley

"In *Polywise's* expansive and eye-opening exploration of the possibilities of nonmonogamous life, Jessica Fern invites us to examine our individual and societal beliefs about love and offers an indispensable guide for newly opened couples' transitions to their next chapter. I am looking forward to recommending this guide to clients and students."
    —Alexandra H. Solomon, PhD, author of *Love Every Day* and host of *Reimagining Love*

Andrea Zanin, MA, is a white, nonbinary, middle-aged queer who lives in Tkaronto (Toronto, Ontario), on the traditional territory of the Mississaugas of the Credit, the Anishnabeg, the Chippewa, the Haudenosaunee and the Wendat peoples. Andrea's writing focuses on queer sex, nonmonogamy and BDSM/Leather. They have written for the *Globe and Mail, The Tyee, Bitch, Ms., Xtra, IN Magazine, Outlooks Magazine* and the *Montreal Mirror*. Their scholarly work, fiction and essays appear in a variety of collections, and they co-authored *More Than Two, Second Edition: Cultivating Nonmonogamous Relationships with Kindness and Integrity* with Eve Rickert. Andrea blogs sporadically at sexgeek.wordpress.com, where they created the ten rules for happy nonmonogamy and coined the term *polynormativity*. Find them on Xitter @sexgeekAZ and Bluesky @andreazanin.bsky.social.